PERSUASIVE WRITING

By Tara McCarthy

SCHOLASTIC
PROFESSIONAL BOOKS

New York • Toronto • London • Auckland • Sydney

Cover design by Vincent Ceci and Jaime Lucero
Interior design by Vincent Ceci and Drew Hires
Interior illustrations by Drew Hires

ISBN 0-590-20934-5

TABLE OF CONTENTS

TO THE TEACHER

Students and adults alike are quick to offer opinions: "It's a great movie!" "You shouldn't do that." "You're wrong." "You're right." As you know, however, an opinion is not persuasive unless it's bolstered by facts and reasons that support it. Assembling and applying these facts and reasons calls upon the higher-level thinking skills of analysis and synthesis. This book is designed to help you help your students use these thinking skills to plan and compose effective pieces of persuasive writing.

BOOK FEATURES

A Gradual Build-Up of Analysis Skills

The three sections of this book lead students from understanding the legitimate elements of persuasion, to recognizing persuasive strategies when we are the audience, and finally to selecting the persuasive approaches that will be most effective in bringing others around to our point of view in different situations.

A Gradual Build-Up of Synthesis Skills

The culminating activity in the book is writing a persuasive essay. To prepare for this challenging and rewarding task, students move along graduated steps: a persuasive sentence here, an informal persuasive paragraph there, a group discussion of TV commercials, opportunities to act out debates orally, invitations to apply what they've just learned to characters in literature and to debates between historical movers-and-doers. Each activity builds upon preceding ones, integrating learned skills with new ones to practice. With lots of synthesizing activities like these under their belt, most students will experience success in writing the essay.

Reproducibles Designed To Build, Not Repeat

Each reproducible page encourages the student to add his or her own particular ideas to a strategy you've discussed with the class as a whole. By completing and organizing the completed pages, the student compiles a unique, individual reference source that reflects his or her own discoveries.

Activities for Students with Various Interests or Modalities

The *Additional Activities* that conclude each Part are designed to appeal to a heterogeneous group of kids. For example, your students who learn best through an aural-oral modality can watch and listen to TV to analyze persuasive techniques, or organize debates on topics that interest them. Students who are visually oriented can analyze posters and photos that "sell" opinions. For your students who learn well through physical activity, there are suggestions for skits and plays in which characters act out their points of view.

GENERAL TEACHING SUGGESTIONS

Use Informal Assessment

Recall that writers learn more about writing from reading their drafts aloud to an audience than they do from any other process. Through these free-reads, most students discover on their own—without audience input—the phrases they wish to keep, change or delete. In addition, as a member of the non-committal audience to the free-read, the teacher can informally pick up and note clues to the student's powers and needs and integrate these clues later on into more formal evaluations.

Have Students Use Writing Folders

While Portfolios represent what the student considers "best," Writing Folders contain "everything." The purpose for keeping everything is that "you-never-know": even the rawest, initial foray into persuasive writing may supply—down the line—the ideas, strong supporting words, or heartfelt statements that inspire or contribute to a polished piece. To help students organize their Writing Folders, supply them with gummed tags on which to write labels, such as *My Partner Profile Ideas*, *Points of View About____(issue)____*, *Commercial Critiques*, and *My Review of the State Fair*.

In general, use the activities in this book as part of your overall design for helping students think, discuss, and write critically about issues that are important to them.

PART ONE

EXPLORING THE ELEMENTS OF PERSUASION

GETTING STARTED

The activities in this section are warm-ups. You can use them to introduce or review the major elements of persuasive writing with your students:

- Stating Opinions
- Using Supporting Facts and Examples
- Connecting Ideas Through Logic and Reasoning
- Appealing to the Target Audience

You can also use the outcomes of the activities to informally assess students' prior knowledge and skill in using these elements.

STATING OPINIONS

Two Points of View

As a start-up, students can use what they know best: themselves.

What You'll Need

For each student, two copies of the reproducible on page 23

Procedure

1. Distribute the reproducible. Students work with a partner.

Each partner lists on one profile page what she or he considers her or his own talents and best qualities, and on the second profile page, the partner's talents and best qualities.

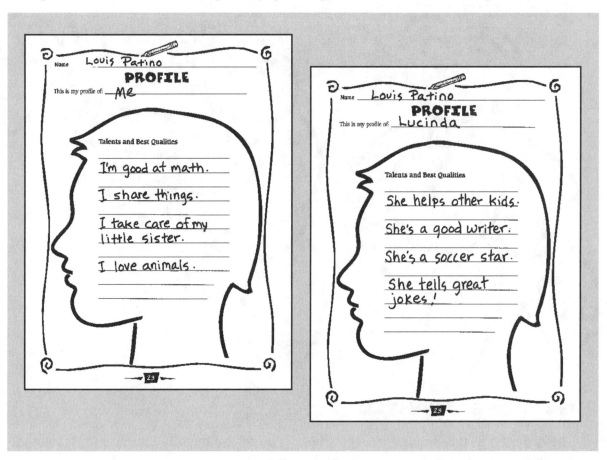

2. Partners exchange partner profile pages, skim to compare them with their own self-profile pages, and then discuss together:

- What two points of view do the two profiles present?
  (my own and my partner's)
- What's different about the profiles? What's the same?
- Is there anything that surprises you in your partner's profile of you?
  Is there anything you disagree with?
- What do you learn by studying another person's view of you?

WRITE

Explain the task: Write two paragraphs. In the first one, use the details from your self-profile. In the second paragraph, use the details from your partner's profile of you. (Teaching Hint: You may wish to suggest a title, such as "All About Me" and a topic sentence for each paragraph, such as: *Here is how I see myself*; *Here is someone else's view of me*.)

Encourage students to imagine a third point of view, such as that of a pet, a parent, or a neighbor, and to write a paragraph from this third viewpoint. (Teaching Hint: Again, you may wish to suggest a topic sentence, such as: *I'm Lucinda's dog, Muffin, and here's my view of Lucinda*.) Suggest that students read their paragraphs aloud to a small group of classmates. This can be a "free-read": The audience listens but doesn't comment. (Writers learn a great deal about writing simply through hearing their own words.)

The Bad Guys Speak!

Through this activity, students expand their ability to consider other opinions and points of view.

Procedure

Have the class brainstorm to list some villains from folk and fairy tales. Examples: Snow White's stepmother; the witch in "Hansel and Gretel"; the giant in "Jack and the Beanstalk"; the wolf in "Little Red Riding Hood." From this list, the class chooses a villain and writes together a paragraph-for-the-chalkboard that tells part of the story from the villain's point of view. Example (the giant):

> A boy named Jack had the nerve to bust into my house! I didn't invite him! There I was, sleeping peacefully in my own home, and this kid breaks in and steals a lot of my stuff! Naturally, I was angry. Naturally, I chased him. Wouldn't you if you got robbed?

Encourage the class to discuss how this alternate point of view helps them to see the old story in a new way.

WRITE

Ask each student to choose another villain from the chalkboard list and relate in writing or by using a tape-recorder a segment of the story from the villain's point of view. (Some students may enjoy writing the entire story from this alternate point of view.) Invite writers to share their work with a group of classmates. How does the new viewpoint add to the audience's understanding of the story?

Identify Different Points of View

This activity is designed to help students identify different points of view, not argue—at this point—for either or any of them.

What You'll Need

Several periodical articles that deal directly with contentions between opposing factions on an issue. Examples: ranchers vs. environmental organizations; NRA members vs. people who want more restrictions on guns; death-penalty advocates vs. groups that oppose the death penalty; groups that want to raise taxes for schools vs. groups that don't.

Procedure

Distribute the different articles to groups of four or five students. Explain the purpose of the activity: (1) determine the issue (what the argument is about); (2) determine the different points of view. Ask groups to read their articles and to discuss what they've determined.

WRITE

1. Each group writes a paragraph that follows this format:

- **1st Sentence:** State what the issue is about.
- **2nd Sentence:** Identify the groups that are debating the issue.
- **3rd Sentence:** Summarize the point of view of one group.
- **4th Sentence:** Summarize the point of view of the other group.

(If there are more than two groups or points of view, write a sentence to summarize each.)

You may wish to present the following example paragraph. Call attention to the use of exact words and phrases (underlined).

> The issue is whether a nuclear power plant should be built on the shore of the Tumble River. The parties discussing the issue are the PowerCenter Corporation and Citizens for Safety. The point of view of the PowerCenter Corporation is that a nuclear power plant would supply customers with inexpensive electric power. The point of view of Citizens for Safety is that nuclear power plants can have accidents that threaten human health.

2. Ask each group to appoint a spokesperson to read the group's paragraph to the class. The audience listens to determine if the issue, contenders, and points of view are presented clearly. A larger question for the audience is, Has the group managed in its paragraph to be objective, that is, to not "take sides"? Groups may wish to revise their paragraphs on the basis of class comments.

3. Ask these open-ended questions:
- Is it hard or easy to present different points of view without stating your personal opinion? Explain.
- On big issues, most of us do have personal opinions. What are some ways of supporting your opinion? Students may suggest using supporting facts and examples.

USING SUPPORTING FACTS AND EXAMPLES

It's a Fact!
Distinguishing between fact and opinion is often a rigorous cognitive task for writers and readers of all ages. The following activity is a warm-up.

What You'll Need
A few different dictionaries and thesauruses; students will need their Partner Profile pages (page 23)

Procedure
1. Ask students to use the dictionaries and thesauruses to find and share definitions of the word *fact*. In general, students will find that *fact* means "something that actually exists and that can be observed and studied objectively." You may wish to present some simple examples from your science or geography curriculum:

- The sun rises in the East and sets in the West.
- Within a cocoon, the butterfly pupa forms wings.
- Mexico is south of the United States.
- Living things in an ecosystem depend on one another.

2. Invite students to present other statements of fact based on what they've learned in their study of science and geography. List students' statements on the chalkboard. Encourage questioning: If students indicate they are not sure that a classmate's statement is a fact, write *Show Me!* after the statement. For example, students are not likely to deny that Mexico is south of the United States, but they may be unsure of a statement such as *Texas was once part of Mexico.*

3. Focus on the chalkoard Show Me! statements. Ask: *What more would you have to know before you accepted this statement as a fact?* (For example—more facts, an explanation, some examples, proof)

4. Ask students to refer to the profiles they made of their partners and to choose one profile item (for example, Lucinda helps other kids) and enter it under Fact, at the center of a Fact-Example Cluster. If the profile item is indeed a fact, the student will be able to supply several supporting examples. On the chalkboard, provide a model.

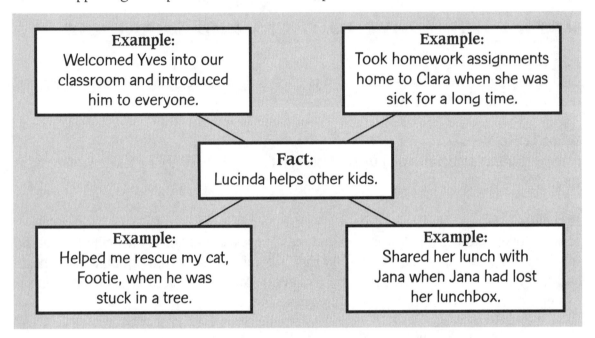

Example:
Welcomed Yves into our classroom and introduced him to everyone.

Example:
Took homework assignments home to Clara when she was sick for a long time.

Fact:
Lucinda helps other kids.

Example:
Helped me rescue my cat, Footie, when he was stuck in a tree.

Example:
Shared her lunch with Jana when Jana had lost her lunchbox.

5. Have students organize their own fact-example clusters based on their Partner Profiles. Establish a rubric: The fact should be supported by at least three examples.

WRITE

Ask students to use their fact-example clusters as a guideline for drafting a persuasive paragraph. Suggest a format:

- **1st Sentence:** State the fact at the center of your cluster.
- **Sentences 2, 3, 4, 5 (etc.):** State the supporting examples.
- **Final Sentence:** State how your fact is supported by your examples.

You may wish to provide a model paragraph that follows the format:

> Lucinda helps other kids. For example, she made a new student, Yves, feel welcome in our classroom. When Clara was sick, Lucinda kept her up-to-date with what was going on at school. Lucinda took time out to help me rescue my cat. When Jana lost her lunchpack, Lucinda was the first to say, "Share my lunch!" All these are examples of how Lucinda is always quick to help other people.

Encourage students to work with a partner to assess their paragraphs, using these questions as discussion guidelines:

- Is the fact stated clearly?
- Do the examples support the fact?
- Do the examples tell about events or situations that can be verified, or checked, by other people?

Students may wish to publish their revised and edited paragraphs by enclosing them in a Class Profiles anthology.

Let's Vote!

Through this activity, students get down to systematically presenting and defending an opinion or point of view.

What You'll Need

Collections of fables, folk tales, fairy tales, myths, and legends with which your students are generally familiar

Procedure

1. On a chalkboard chart, list major qualities of characters in folk literature, and provide one example character. Ask the class to suggest at least one other character who has this quality. Example:

Quality	Example Characters
Scary!	• the giant in "Jack and the Beanstalk" • the witch in "Hansel and Gretel" • the wolf in "Little Red Riding Hood"
Greedy!	• Rumplestiltskin • the fox in "The Fox and the Grapes" • Bre'r Rabbit
Strong!	• Hercules • Paul Bunyan • Diana the Huntress
Lucky!	• the Frog Prince • Cinderella • Jack in "Jack and the Beanstalk"

2. Divide the class into eight groups. Assign each Quality (for example, Lucky) to two groups. Each group chooses the character from the chart who they think best exemplifies this quality (for example, Luckiest: Cinderella) and then lists examples to support their choice. Encourage groups to use the literature collection to find ideas and incidents that support their choices. Example:

Cinderella is lucky ...
- to have a Fairy Godmother
- that the prince falls in love with her
- that she loses a shoe as a clue to her identity
- that the prince works so hard to find her

WRITE

Have each student draft a persuasive paragraph based on his or her group's discussion. Example:

WHY YOU SHOULD VOTE FOR
<u>Cinderella</u> as <u>Luckiest</u>

Cinderella is a lucky character, because everything happens to her by accident. First of all, she is lucky enough to have a fairy godmother who can send her to the ball. Then the Prince just happens to fall in love with Cinderella. Then, by a lucky accident, she loses one of her shoes. Luckily, the Prince is a person who is determined to find the woman whom the shoe fits. By luck, he stops by Cinderella's house, tries the shoe, and sees that it fits. Without all these lucky events, Cinderella might still be brushing up cinders in her stepmother's house!

Ask each group to study members' drafts and decide on the most persuasive points in each. Group editors can write a final draft. Then the group appoints a reader to present the paragraph to the class. After listening to the paragraphs of both groups, the audience members comment on which of the two paragraphs is most persuasive and tell why they think so.

Groups may wish to revise their paragraphs based on ideas they've garnered through audience response.

LOGIC AND REASONING

Order, Please!

Most students like the words *logic* and *logical*. This activity builds on students' fondness for these terms to show how a logical argument is one that presents related ideas in sequence.

Procedure

1. Copy the paragraph below on the chalkboard. Explain that the first sentence states the writer's opinion, but that the other sentences are out of order: that is, they don't follow logical sequence.

> **(1)** Animal shelters are overcrowded because many pet owners are irresponsible. **(2)** They bring these animals to the shelter. **(3)** For example, a family may buy a cat or dog without thinking ahead of time about the care the animal requires. **(4)** Many abandoned pets have to be put to sleep there because of the thoughtlessness of their original owners. **(5)** Or the owner may fail to get the pet neutered and then become upset by an unwelcome litter of kittens or puppies.

2. Read the paragraph aloud to the class. Then ask students to discuss how to re-order sentences 2–5 so that one idea leads logically to the next. An example: 1,3,5,2,4. Responses may vary somewhat, and that's fine! The objective here is simply to get kids focused on the importance of presenting an argument through steps that the audience can easily follow.

WRITE

Distribute the copies of the reproducible. Ask students to work independently or with a partner to rewrite the paragraph to make it logical, using what they've learned from the class discussion. Invite students to read their paragraphs aloud. Teaching Hint: You might make this a "free-read." Explain the strategy to students: In a free-read, the audience does not comment. Rather, the writer alone decides—from listening to her/his own oral reading—what to add, delete, or change.

What Are Your Reasons?

This activity helps students understand how a logical, convincing argument grows out of the writer's careful assembly of supporting facts.

Procedure

On the chalkboard, present the first and last sentences (the statement of opinion and the conclusion) of a persuasive paragraph on a topic with which most of your students are familiar. Leave a lot of space between these sentences. Work with students to supply and write supporting facts and reasons that lead logically, step-by-step, from the first sentence to the last sentence. Example:

If you are a passenger in a car driven by a drunk driver, your life is in danger. (Examples: Drunk drivers have a hard time adjusting speed to road conditions. They take dangerous chances. They forget or ignore safety rules. Often, drunk drivers forget their responsibilty to keep passengers safe. Thousands of people each year are killed by drunk drivers.) **For these reasons, you should not ride in a car with a driver who has had too much to drink.**

WRITE

Invite students to use what they've just learned about supplying reasons and logical order to rough-draft persuasive paragraphs on other topics about behaviors your community generally agrees are important to consider in school. According to your discretion, these topics might include volatile ones such as: accepting invitations from strangers, experimenting with drugs, playing with guns, smoking; or less volatile topics such as adopting healthy diets, getting adequate physical exercise, or making provisions for day-care for little kids whose parents work away from home.

For optimal results, ask students to share their drafts with partners who've written on a similar subject. Partners can assess opening sentences, supporting facts, logical links, and conclusions. They can then use what they've learned to revise their drafts.

Ideas That Don't Belong
In their writing activities through the grades, students have been learning how to recognize and delete ideas and sentences that don't stick to the subject. Through the following activity, students practice applying this understanding to persuasive paragraphs.

What You'll Need
For each student, a copy of the reproducible on page 24; a copy of the same reproducible to show on the overhead projector

Procedure
1. Show the reproducible on the overhead, and focus on the first example. Call attention to the opening and concluding sentences, and invite students to tell from these two sentences what the writer's opinion is on the subject of School Lunches. (Sample response: *Kids should be able to choose between meals prepared by school cooks and "fast-food" meals brought in from outside.*) Then ask students to find the two sentences that have nothing to do with/do not support/distract attention from this point of view (sentences 4 and 7) and discuss why they don't fit/don't help to develop the writer's opinion. (For example, what one's parents like to eat at movies, and who founded BurgerBelly, have nothing to do with what kids like to eat at school.)

2. Distribute the copies of the reproducible. Ask students to cross out the sentences in the first paragraph that the class has decided don't belong. Ask a volunteer to read the revised paragraph aloud. Review with the class: *What is the writer's opinion, and what ideas support it?*

WRITE

Ask students to work independently to read the second paragraph on the reproducible, find the two sentences that don't belong (sentences 3 and 6), and delete them as they rewrite the paragraph on a separate sheet of paper. Have students follow-up by discussing their decisions and rewriting with a small group of classmates.

THINKING ABOUT YOUR AUDIENCE

Analyzing Different Viewpoints

One goal of persuasive writing is to bring an "undecided" audience around to the writer's point of view. A second goal of the writer—more difficult to achieve—is to convince an audience with an opinion contrary to the writer's to "switch sides." In the latter case, the writer's first step is to understand why the target audience holds that opinion.

What You'll Need

For each student, a copy of the reproducible on page 25

Procedure

1. If your students have done the activities for Stating Opinions (pages 8-9), briefly review with them what they learned. Examples:

- Different people may look at the same situation in different ways.
- There may be a lot of different opinions on the same subject.

2. Distribute the reproducible and preview the tasks and directions. Discuss what it means to be objective: to consider all the ideas that relate to a situation without stating your personal opinions. You may wish to have the class work together to complete #1. Example:

Should our school have snack and soda machines in the cafeteria?

• YES.
Reasons: 1. Many students get hungry in the middle of the afternoon and need a place to get snacks. **2.** Some students may not like the lunches offered by the school cafeteria. **3.** Visitors to our school might appreciate snack and soda machines when they get hungry or thirsty.

• NO.
Reasons: 1. Most vending-machine food is not nutritious and has a high sugar content. **2.** Vending-machine snacks and drinks are not economical because they usually cost much more than they do in stores. **3.** There may be more litter around the school from people discarding wrappers, packages, and bottles carelessly.

---

3. Ask students to work with partners to complete Part #2 of the reproducible. Partner-groups can then get together to compare and discuss their work, using these basic criteria:

- Have we presented the same number—or almost the same number—of reasons for the the YES and the NO sides?
- Have we done a pretty good job of keeping our own personal feelings and opinions out of our lists? A good test: From our list, can you tell where we stand on the issue? (Best answer: NO)

WRITE

Ask partners to use the ideas on their list to develop a paragraph presenting the YES and NO sides. Writing guidelines:

- The topic sentence rewords the original question to make it a statement.
- The follow-up sentences state the pro and con reasons objectively.

You may wish to present an example:

Students have different opinions about whether our school cafeteria should have snack and soda machines. Many students feel that the machines are necessary for kids who get hungry in the middle of the afternoon or for kids who don't like cafeteria lunches. Pro-machine students also think that school visitors would appreciate the machines. However, many other students are against having vending machines in the school. These students note that the snacks and sodas are not nutritional, have a lot of sugar in them, and are very expensive. Anti-machine students also feel that vending machines are a possible source of litter around our school.

Have partners read their paragraphs aloud. The audience listens to assess the paragraphs, based on the criteria above.

- Is the issue stated clearly in the first sentence?
- Are the pro and con positions stated clearly and given "equal time"?
- Is the paragraph objective? That is, does it avoid telling what side of the argument the writers favor?

Partners may wish to revise their paragraphs on the basis of the class critique.

COMPOSITION SKILL

Using Transitional Words

1. On the chalkboard, list some transitional words and phrases that writers use when they're presenting opposing ideas.

- although
- though
- the reverse
- but
- unlike
- while
- however
- yet
- unless
- in contrast
- on the other hand

2. Explain that transitional words are used to show how ideas are connected. Provide some examples:

- Many people feel that gun laws should be stricter, but many other people feel that the gun laws we have are strict enough.
- Unlike most of my classmates, I believe that students should be given more homework.
- Families on vacation want to visit national parks, yet many of these parks are damaged by an overload of tourist traffic.
- While many people argue that capital punishment cuts down on crime, other people argue the reverse, that it doesn't cut down on crime at all.

3. Supply some sentence frames and ask the class to provide transitional words and phrases from the chalkboard list. Examples:

- Some school-board members believe that schools should be in session all year around; (<u>however</u> or <u>but</u>) most students and many teachers oppose the idea.
- The Shop-o-Rama Company plans to build another mall nearby, (<u>although</u> or <u>though</u>) their present mall has many empty shops.
- A weekend curfew for teenagers might make our town quieter at night; (<u>on the other hand</u>, <u>but</u>, or <u>however</u>), a curfew might violate young people's rights.
- My mom thinks billboards are an ugly blight on the landscape. (<u>In contrast</u> or <u>On the other hand</u>), my dad believes billboards are helpful to travelers and to local businesses.
- Students should not have to do homework (<u>unless</u>) they haven't completed their work in class.

4. Ask students to copy the chalkboard list of transitional words and phrases, put the list in their Writing Folders, and use it as they revise and edit their persuasive writing.

1. Write a Declaration

If your students are studying United States history, show a copy of the Declaration of Independence on the overhead projector and call students' attention to the last sentences of the second paragraph.

> "The history of the present King of Great Britain is a history of repeated injuries and usurpations, all having in direct object the establishment of an absolute tyranny over these States. To prove this, let facts be submitted to a candid world."

Have students count the number of facts and examples that the writer of the Declaration, Thomas Jefferson, submitted (27!). Ask: (1) *How do all these facts and examples support the point of view that an absolute tyranny was being established?* (2) *How might the examples have helped to convince colonists who were "undecided" to adopt Jefferson's point of view?*

Invite students to write a Declaration on an issue they're immediately concerned with in school or at home. Establish guidelines:

- The first part of the Declaration should present the student's point of view.
- The next part of the Declaration should present at least three facts that support the point of view.
- The last part of the Declaration should suggest a solution.

You may wish to present an example:

> (**Point of View**): As a student, I hold these truths to be self-evident: that kids want worthwhile activities after school and that our community has failed to establish these activities.
>
> To prove this, let these facts be presented to a candid community. (**Facts**): So far, the town has not built the Student Recreation Center that was promised in the last election. Also, the school has failed to set up an after-school Study Room. In addition, community organizations have failed to invite kids to participate in out-reach work like helping out in soup-kitchens. (**Solution**): We students propose to start an organization called **WIN** (**W**hen **I**n **N**eed). WIN will be a clearing-house that directs students to valuable things they can do for themselves and for other people.

Have students work in groups of five or six to listen to classmates' Declarations, determine whether the guidelines have been met, and—if necessary—suggest changes or additions. Then suggest that each student revise her or his draft to incorporate group comments that the student finds helpful. Post Declarations on a bulletin board under the head **Let Me Persuade You.**

2. Study Opinions of Book Characters

Ask Book-Talk Groups to read (or re-read) novels or chapter books set in the time of the American Revolution in which main characters start off with one point of view or opinion, then change, amend, or bolster their opinion as the story progresses. After reading, the group can share ideas about what events or ideas affected the main characters' opinions. You may want to invite groups to present their book-talks as round-table discussions to hold before the class. Recommended books for this activity:

- Avi. *The Fighting Ground* (Lippincott, 1984)
- Brady, Esther Wood. *Toliver's Secret* (Crown, 1976)
- Collier, James Lincoln, and Christopher Collier. *My Brother Sam Is Dead* (Four Winds, 1974)
- Griffin, Judith Berry. *Phoebe and the General* (Coward, 1977)
- McGovern, Ann. *The Secret Soldier: The Story of Deborah Sampson* (Four Winds, 1987)

3. From Numbers to Words

Ask students to look through newspapers and magazines to find and reproduce charts or graphs that illustrate poll results of public opinion on a current problem, issue, or debate. Show the charts/graphs on the overhead projector. Discuss: the question or questions poll respondents had to answer; what different opinions the visual shows; how answers are shown in the visual; what opinion the plurality of respondents hold.

Have the class work together to compose a paragraph that summarizes the opinions shown in a graph or chart. Remind students that the first sentence should state what the issue is. Examples:

- People who live in public housing have different opinions about whether residents should be allowed to keep dogs.
- There's a big debate going on about whether our schools should require students to wear uniforms.

Some students will enjoy the challenge of conducting their own opinion-surveys about a current school or community issue. Discuss: *How will you phrase the questions so that they are clear? Whom will you interview to make sure you get a variety of opinions?*

How will you tabulate or record answers? How will you show the results on a graph or chart? Students can share the results of their surveys by showing and discussing their resultant visuals, and/or by writing a summary of their findings.

4. Just Listen to That!
As an activity to carry out with families at home, students can watch and listen to one of the regularly scheduled discussion-debate TV programs to assess the persuasion skills of the participants.

To facilitate the activity, give each student a copy of the reproducible on page 26 and preview the data they are to provide. In class, you may want to have students scan TV schedules and determine which debate programs they'll watch and listen to at home.

Back in the classroom, students can share and discuss their completed TV discussion analyses. Discussion questions: *What makes an argument "good," that is, helpful to an audience that wants to know all about an issue? What makes an argument "bad," that is, confusing or distracting or incomplete?*

Students who've watched the same program may enjoy the challenge of reenacting the TV discussion to improve it. They may make the topic, the points of view, and the supporting details clearer; stick to the subject; correct any "bad manners" the TV disputants showed, such as interrupting other speakers, making faces, or "calling people names." Provide rehearsal time and, if you have a Camcorder, ask groups to use it to record their discussions so that they and their classmates can critique them later on.

Name _____

PROFILE

This is my profile of: _____

Talents and Best Qualities

_____

_____

_____

_____

_____

_____

_____

_____

_____

_____

IDEAS THAT DON'T BELONG

1. Read the paragraph. Cross out the sentences that don't help to develop the opinion stated in the first sentence.

(1) Kids want a lot of choices at lunchtime. (2) The cafeteria cooks do a good job of appealing to kids who want a really well-balanced meal. (3) But some kids just want snacks like the ones that BurgerBelly sells—snacks like Potato Puffies, BabyBurgs, and Icey-Ikes. (4) My parents always buy a sack of Potato Puffies to eat at the movies. (5) Our school should make both kinds of meals available. (6) Let's persuade our local BurgerBelly to sell food at lunchtime in our cafeteria. (7) BurgerBelly was founded by R. U. Hungry, of Portly, Arkansas. (8) Then we would all be able to choose between cafeteria meals and fast-food snacks.

2. Read the paragraph. Find the two sentences that don't belong. On a separate sheet of paper, rewrite the paragraph, leaving out the sentences that don't belong.

(1) Every student in our school should have an opportunity to participate in Field Day. (2) Many students want to compete in the events, such as the races, hurdles, and broad jumps. (3) In ancient Rome, athletic competitions were very important and festive occasions. (4) However, other kids would rather not compete, but would like to contribute to Field Day in other ways. (5) These students could make and hand out programs, announce events, or serve as judges. (6) We all like to watch the Olympic Games on television. (7) With careful planning, we can make sure that all of us have an important role in making Field Day successful.

Name _____

ANALYZING DIFFERENT VIEWPOINTS

1. Students in one school are debating this issue:

Should our school have snack and soda machines in the cafeteria?

Some students say "Yes." Some students say "No." In the chart, list some reasons to support each side of the debate.

Y E S Reasons:

_____
_____
_____
_____
_____
_____

N O Reasons:

_____
_____
_____
_____
_____
_____

2. Choose one of the questions below. On a separate sheet of paper, list reasons to support **YES** answers and reasons to support **NO** answers. Strive for the same number of reasons in each list.

* Should our school have a no-homework policy?

* Should every student be required to learn a foreign language?

* Should students in our school wear uniforms?

* Should students repeat a grade if they don't pass final tests?

* Should students be able to skip a grade if their school work is outstanding?

Name _____

JUST LISTEN TO THAT!

Name of Program I Watched: _____

Date: _____ Time: _____ Channel: _____

Participants   Their Titles, Jobs, or Background

_____   _____

_____   _____

_____   _____

_____   _____

_____   _____

What was the Big Issue that the speakers discussed?

_____

_____

Grade the participants:

• Who was best at sticking to the point? _____

• Who was vague or said things that had little to do with the issue?

_____

• Did any of the participants have "bad manners" such as interrupting, making faces, or attacking the personality of an opponent? If so, give an example.

_____

_____

What was the most important thing you learned about …

• the issue that the speakers were debating? _____

• how to (or how not to) present opinions? _____

PART TWO

ANALYZING PERSUASIVE TECHNIQUES

GETTING STARTED

As students become familiar with the basic elements of persuasion presented in Part One, they grow in their ability to analyze the persuasive messages that they see, hear, and read almost every day. Are the ideas in these messages presented logically? Are the ideas supported by facts and examples? Who is the target audience, and what special techniques are used to appeal to this audience?

Prepare for Part Two by setting up a classroom reference collection of mail-order catalogs and advertising flyers. Enlist student assistance in building this collection. If possible, also make a videotape of several TV commercials that use the techniques presented in the following pages. Ask students to use and build the collection as they carry out the activities in this section.

GET ON THE BANDWAGON!

Write a Bandwagon Ad

You may want to begin by telling students what a *bandwagon* is: a highly decorated parade float crowded with enthusiastic participants in an event (for example, clowns, musicians, political figures).

Procedure

1. Write the following statements on the chalkboard. (Don't use underlining yet; students will supply it.) Ask students to read the statements aloud and identify the words or phrases that suggest that "everyone who's smart and hip knows this/is doing this." Call on a volunteer to underline the bandwagon words and phrases that classmates identify.

- Get into the jeans with the Glow! <u>Up-to-date kids</u> proudly wear that Glow Jeans glow-stripe day and night!
- <u>Everyone</u> is collecting them! Are you? Buy the latest Fluffy Friend before <u>millions of collectors</u> have bought out our entire supply!
- What's the <u>favorite</u> after-school snack? <u>Nine out of ten kids</u> rush home to gobble up the all-time, <u>all-around winner</u>, Sniggle Bars.
- <u>People in-the-know</u> are switching to Pasta-Paste, the toothpaste that <u>hundreds of dentists recommend</u> because it tastes like spaghetti.

2. Help students get involved in a lively debate of the issues raised by the words and phrases they've identified:

- How do the words and phrases make the audience feel that they absolutely must buy the product?
- What details—if any—are supplied to show the source of figures such as *everyone*, *people-in-the-know*, *nine-out-of-ten* and, *hundreds of dentists*?
- Is a product that's a best-seller necessarily better than a product that isn't quite as popular? For example, is Pasta-Paste a better tooth-cleaner than other brands?
- What is a fad? (an interest followed with enthusiasm for a very short time) How do the ads appeal to fads? Ask the class to recall fads they followed and products they wanted or bought in earlier grades, but that are now out-of-date.
- What are the advantages and disadvantages of getting on the bandwagon?

WRITE

Have the class brainstorm for a chalkboard list of generic items. Each student then chooses an item, gives it an original brand name, and writes an ad that uses the bandwagon technique of persuasion.

Invite students to read their ads aloud in a "persuasive" voice. In addition, or as an alternate activity, the student might draw a bandwagon for the product, featuring the persuasive words and phrases. Examples:

Product	My Name for the Product
sneakers	Leap 'n Stride
book bag	PackaBook
cereal	Inner-Gees
skates	Speedy Demons
candy	Bubble Pops

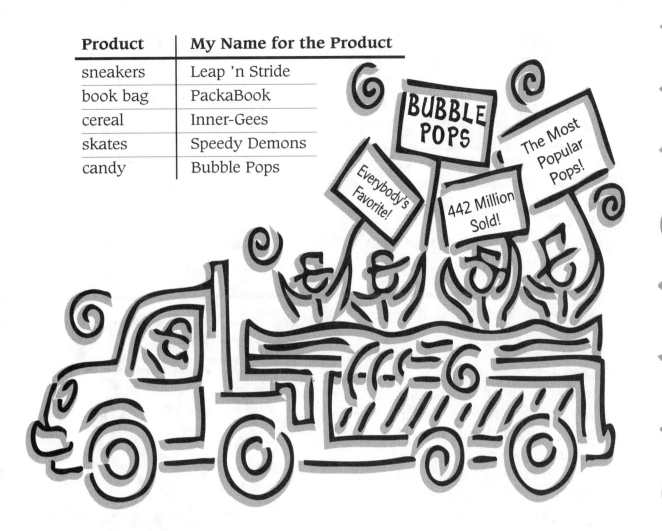

TESTIMONIALS:
THE FAMOUS-PEOPLE TECHNIQUE

Write a Commercial Script

Almost every student will be able to come up with examples of TV commercials that feature a famous person—for example, sports stars speaking for makers of sporting goods; TV and movie actors featured in ads for telephone services.

Procedure

Ask the class to name some products/services that use a famous spokesperson to testify to the "greatness" of the product or service. List students' examples on the chalkboard. Then use the following discussion questions:

- Why do advertisers use famous people in ad campaigns? (The audience admires superstars and thinks "If she/he says it's good, it must be!"
- In which ads might the spokesperson actually be an expert in the kind of product advertised? (For example, a basketball star might know a lot about sports shoes.) In which ads is the spokesperson unlikely to know a great deal about the product or service? (For example, a TV actor might not know much more than the rest of us do about competing telephone services.)

• What's the usual reason that famous people act as spokespersons for a product or service? (They get paid for doing so.)

• There are occasions in which famous people donate (don't charge for) their testimony for charitable causes such as raising money for war victims, for feeding hungry children, or for fighting diseases. Ask students to view, listen for, and read ads for testimonies like these. Why might people donate their time for this kind of work? (They truly believe in the cause they speak for; they want audience donations to go to the cause, not to a fee for the spokesperson.)

WRITE

Ask students to write a testimonial for a product or service they want an audience to buy, use, or contribute to. Here are the steps:

• Choose a product, service, or charity that you want to sell. The product or service can be a real one, or one that you've made up during your bandwagon activity (pages 28–29).

• Decide on a real-life super-star to be a spokesperson for your company or cause. Why would this person be especially effective as a persuader?

• Write a short paragraph for the spokesperson to say to the audience. The paragraph might open with an identifying lead-in—for example, "You probably recognize me as the eight-time winner of the All-Star trophy."

• Encourage students to use some bandwagon words and phrases in the testimonial.

Suggest to students that they read the drafts of their advertising paragraphs aloud to a small group of classmates. Set up directed-listening guidelines:

• Listen to identify the famous spokesperson and the product or service he or she is advertising.

• Listen for persuasive words and phrases.

• Be ready to suggest some ways to strengthen the testimonial, if the writer asks you to do this.

Students may enjoy publishing their ads by showing them as dialogue balloons set in picture panels.

GLITTERING GENERALITIES

Backing Up Generalities with Facts

This activity not only helps students recognize vague, general terms but also encourages them to be specific in their own writing and speaking.

Procedure

1. Ahead of time, prepare a two-column chalkboard chart, and list the words and phrases in the first column.

Glittering Generality	Our Questions
better	better than what?
more powerful	as compared to what?
new, improved	newer than what? improved over what?
most popular	most popular with whom?
healthy, nutritious	What makes it "healthy" and "nutritious"?
satisfied customers	Who are they? How many of them are there? How do we know they're satisfied?

2. Explain that a *generality* is a vague word, phrase, or statement, and that a *glittering generality* is one that has a feel-good quality to it, as do the items in the first column. Ask students to use logic and their critical-thinking skills to come up with questions that a savvy consumer might ask on hearing or reading persuasive ads like the following (possible responses are listed in the second column).

3. Have the class work together to rewrite one of the glittering-generality ads in **2** to make it more specific. Write the class's revision on the chalkboard. Examples:

- Wild Ranger is more powerful than our competitors' Road Rogue and Hill Honcho, because Wild Ranger has four-wheel drive, an eight-cylinder engine, and all-terrain wheels and tires. These features make Wild Ranger the most popular vehicle among 100 drivers we polled in our comparison test drive of all three vehicles.
- We've improved Tooth-Saver by placing the bristles so that they really slant-in on those hard-to-reach spots. This new design can help you remove plaque from all your teeth.

Chock-o-Mints are the better after-school snack!

Wild Ranger—more powerful, most popular on the highway!

Satisfied customers gobble up healthy, nutritious Beebee's Breakfast Bonanzas!

New, improved Tooth-Saver! Buy it today!

WRITE

Ask students to work independently or with a partner to write an ad or commercial that uses glittering generalities and backs them up with specific details. For ideas, students can refer to the chalkboard chart and to your classroom collection of catalogs, flyers, and videotaped commercials.

As a warm-up or prerevision activity, you may wish to present the Composition Skill on page 38, *Using Exact Words*.

Invite students to read their ads and commercials aloud to a group of classmates. The audience can listen to identify the generalities and the supporting details. What makes the writer's ad persuasive to a savvy audience? What more would the audience like to know about the product or service? Writers may wish to incorporate some audience suggestions into their final drafts.

Publishing ideas:

- Post final copies on a **Buy Us!** bulletin board.
- Have students move onto the next activity, TRANSFER, then combine what they learn there with the persuasive paragraphs they've written here.

TRANSFER: PICTURES AND SLOGANS THAT PERSUADE

Design a Print Ad

Through this activity, students can come to realize the persuasive power of visual symbols and catchwords and catchphrases.

What You'll Need

For each student, a copy of the reproducible on page 42; a copy of the same reproducible to show on an overhead projector; your collection of catalogs, flyers, and tapes

Procedure

1. Show page 42 on the overhead. Ask students to quickly brainstorm what comes to mind when they see the symbols or read the catchwords and catchphrases in column 1. Write students' responses in the second column. Examples:

2. With the class, discuss what *transfer* means in persuasive writing: using a strong pictorial symbol or general phrase that arouses the audience's emotions so that they'll connect—transfer—the emotion to the product being sold. Point out that transfer techniques appeal to universal feelings—for example, happiness, fear, patriotism, urgency, wanting to be rich, love of animals. Discuss how the chart examples show an appeal to emotions.

3. Distribute the reproducibles of page 43. Divide the class into four or five groups. Each group studies the classroom collection of persuasive ads and commercials. For column 2, each group enters at least one example of a picture or catchphrase that appeals to the emotion. For column 3, the group enters the product or service that the advertiser is selling. Have a group scribe write or draw the groups' best examples on a copy of the chart to show to the whole class on the overhead projector. Discuss the entries and what's persuasive about them. Examples:

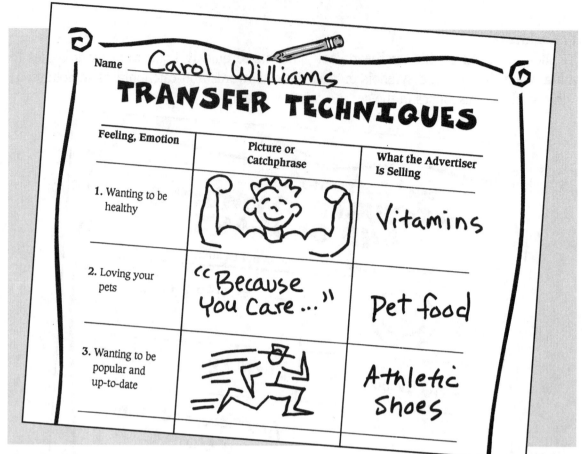

Name Carol Williams

TRANSFER TECHNIQUES

Feeling, Emotion	Picture or Catchphrase	What the Advertiser Is Selling
1. Wanting to be healthy		Vitamins
2. Loving your pets	"Because You Care..."	Pet food
3. Wanting to be popular and up-to-date		Athletic Shoes

WRITE

Ask students to work independently or with a partner to write/design an ad that might appear in print or that might be the script for a Web site entry or for a famous person's TV-commercial testimonial.

• Establish guidelines through a pre-writing discussion:
  •• Decide on the goods or service you want to persuade your audience to buy.
  •• Appeal to audience emotions:
    ••• Design a visual symbol: a picture or design that arouses the audience's feelings and needs.
    ••• Use a beginning catchphrase: a phrase or sentence also designed to capture audience attention.
  •• Supply details to tell the audience how your product or service may answer their needs.

• Encourage students to try to sell not only ordinary, realistic goods and services, but also bizarre and unusual ones. Examples:
  •• odd socks found in other people's laundry
  •• weather phenomena: hurricanes, rainbows, thunderstorms
  •• qualities, such as kindness, ambition, truthfulness
  •• strange products, such as chocolate-flavored pasta, TV sets that don't work, or cars or homes without windows
  •• expeditions to uncomfortable places: sub-zero temperatures, areas where hostile native peoples attempt to kill intruders, planets where there is no water

You may wish to present an example on the chalkboard or overhead projector:

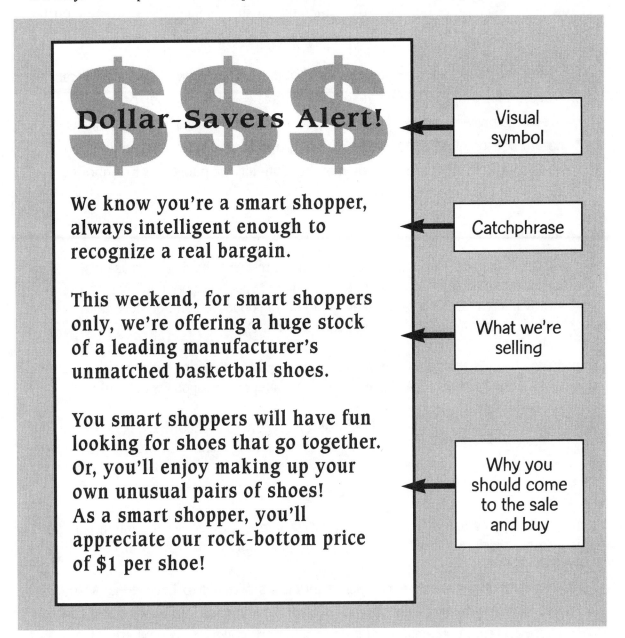

To publish, students can arrange a "For Sale" display on a bulletin board. Classmates can study the ads to determine how well advertisers have followed the guidelines on page 34. Which ads are persuasive enough to attract a savvy audience? What makes these ads convincing?

CARD-STACKING

What's Your Angle?

Card-stacking means giving the positive side for your own point of view but none of the positive points for your opponent's position. Card-stacking is not only a common advertising strategy but also one that young people themselves use frequently as they argue for something they want.

Procedure

1. Ahead of time, write the following paragraph on the chalkboard or to show on the overhead projector.

> Residents of big apartment projects should not be allowed to have dogs. Dogs that are unfriendly or vicious may attack and hurt other people who live in the project and use the open spaces around it. Dogs are also a health-hazard because they dirty the grass, playgrounds, and sidewalks. In addition, dogs that bark and whine a lot make it difficult for people in neighboring apartments to sleep and work.

Have a student read the paragraph aloud. Then ask:

- What is the writer's opinion about apartment residents having dogs as pets?
- How many reasons does the writer provide to support the opinion? (3)
- How many reasons does the writer give for the opposite point of view, that residents *should* be allowed to own dogs? (none)

Explain to students the term *card-stacking*: giving the supporting reasons for your own point of view, and few or none of the reasons that support the opposite point of view.

2. Ask groups of five or six students to use the reference collection (see page 27) to find at least two ads or commercials that use the card-stacking technique. Groups then present the examples to the class for discussion and analysis.

WRITE

Return to the paragraph in 1 above. Ask the class to work together to write a paragraph in which the cards are stacked in favor of being allowed to keep dogs. Example:

> Residents of big apartment projects should be allowed to have dogs. Many older people who live alone rely on dogs for companionship. Also, a dog can act as protection against intruders. In addition, children everywhere have a right to the fun and learning that comes from raising and caring for a dog.

Invite partners to read their completed paragraphs aloud to the class. Are both arguments equally persuasive? Why or why not?

THINKING ABOUT YOUR AUDIENCE

Choosing an Appropriate Tone

For persuasive writers, *tone* means the style or manner of expression we use in addressing the target audience. For example, a tone may be informal, or formal; playful, or serious; somber, or hopeful.

Procedure

1. Copy the following chart on the chalkboard, or reproduce it for use on the overhead projector.

What I'm Selling: Full-o-Life Vitamin Tablets

AUDIENCE	MEDIA	SCRIPT OR AD COPY
1. Doctors	A magazine that physicians subscribe to	Plubsome Laboratories' years of success shows doctors' confidence in our products. Now you will want to suggest our Full-o-Life tablets to your patients who suffer from Lazy-Osis, Can't-Do-Itis, and Couchess-Potato-Itis Syndrome.
2. Kids	TV	Get up and go! Knock 'em dead! Full-o-Life Vitamins turn you into a winner. Astound your friends with your bursts of Full-o-Life energy!
3. Families	newspaper ad	Is your child listless? Does he or she sit around all afternoon? As a responsible caregiver, have you considered that your child may have a vitamin deficiency? Think of Full-o-Life! You owe it to your child!

2. Define *tone* for students (see page 36). Ask the class to identify the tones in column 3 of the chart and how they appeal to the target audiences—for example, (1) formal, professional tone to appeal to expert doctors; (2) playful, fun tone to appeal to kids who like physical competition; (3) anxious, concerned tone to appeal to adults who worry a lot about their kids.

WRITE

Ask students to work independently or with a partner to write two ads for one of the following products. The tone of their ads should appeal to the two different designated audiences. Writers read their ads to a group of classmates. The audience listens to identify the tone and the probable audience for the ad.

Product	Audiences
1. Plaque-Away Tooth Gel	Dentists, Kids
2. Seismo Gorgeous (a new car)	Families with kids, Drivers who want to be up-to date
3. Quacky-Snacks (a snack food for parrots)	People who own parrots. parrots
4. Rosy Foam (a liquid soap)	Doctors who are concerned about their patients' hygiene, People who want to smell good
5. Bungey Boos (collectible stuffed toys)	Kids who like to collect stuff, Relatives wondering what to give as birthday gifts

As a follow-up, ask students to use your classroom collection to identify ads designed to appeal to certain audiences, and that use an appropriate tone for doing so.

COMPOSITION SKILL

Using Exact Words

1. Ahead of time, draw the following web on the chalkboard. Provide room for writing lines as shown, but don't write the underlined phrases (they're examples of what students might suggest through discussion in step 2).

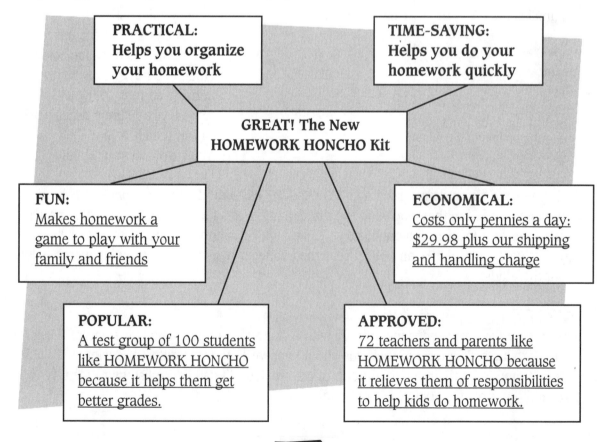

2. Help the class identify the general words in the web (those in capital letters), then the specific, exact phrases that tell why Homework Honcho is practical and time-saving. Ask students to suggest phrases that would make the other web entries more exact. Prompts: *With whom could you make Homework Honcho a fun game? What might "shipping charges" amount to, and would these charges still make Homework Honcho "economical"? How many students were in the test group and in what way did Homework Honcho help them? How many teachers and parents approved Homework Honcho, and from what responsibilities did it relieve them?* Enter students' responses into the web. Sample responses are underlined.

3. Show the following chart on the chalkboard or on the overhead projector. For each pair, ask students to identify the ad that will be more appealing to a savvy audience and to explain their choice.

Basketball Bouncers are great!	Basketball Bouncers are durable, support your feet, and meet the newest standards for hip kids' design.
Wizard Electronics will refund your purchase price and add a 50% bonus if you find a lower price in a competing store.	Visit Wizard Electronics for low prices and friendly service. After all, we've been your neighbor for 27 years!
Go with the Glow that never fades! A built-in recharger automatically repowers your Glowworm flashlight when the batteries run low.	Everybody wants to conquer the Glow-Light Glowworm. But nobody can beat the Glowworm for dependability. Go with the Glowworm!

4. Ask students to work independently or with a partner to write a persuasive ad or commercial for one of the following products or services. For students' references to exact words, you may want to supply dictionaries and thesauruses.

- YoBar Candy: a candy bar that has some vitamins in it
- Lino Hypes: in-line skates with a hand-controlled emergency brake and pedestrian-warning beeper
- Future Fantasies: a CD-ROM program that shows you what your adult life may be like, based on what you're doing now
- Scholar Services: a business that provides students with mentors who help with school work and homework
- Gorgeous People: a business that claims to make any client totally beautiful or handsome

To publish, students can post their ads on a bulletin board or work together to set up ads as they would appear in the Classified Advertisements section of a newspaper.

ADDITIONAL ACTIVITIES

1. Impossible Ads: Unstacking the Cards

Ask students to imagine that advertisers actually wanted to present not only the best qualities of their own product but also the best qualities of their competitor's product. Present and discuss the following example. Then ask students to work independently or with two or three partners to amend, or add to, an ad they've written so as to include a competitor's selling points.

> Movie Munches are the crunchiest, yummiest chocolate snacks you'll ever find for chomping on at your local CinePlex. You chocolate lovers will adore our melty, down-home, silk-on-your-tongue flavor. On the other hand, if you don't like chocolate, or are allergic to it, buy a bunch of our competitor's Viewer Veggies. These wholesome snacks are chocolate-free and are made out of nourishing broccoli and sun-dried tomatoes.

2. Book Blurbs

Share with students some of the testimonials that appear on the backs of book jackets. Discuss how these blurbs, though brief, help to sell the book to customers by using persuasive words and phrases. Ask students who have enjoyed the same book to write blurbs for the book's jacket.

Words of Praise for...

FARLEY GROFFET, MAN OF MYSTERY

"The best book I've ever read about searching for the bones of ancient lizards."
—*Samantha Greensea*

"Groffet's achievements are truly unusual."
—*Wyn Summ*

"A book to put on your shelf along with the author's other book FARLEY GROFFET, HEROIC EXPLORER."
—*Laura Reeder*

Students may also enjoy completing the book jacket with a front fold that entices readers with an illustration of an exciting incident in the story and with the book title lettered in an intriguing way.

3. Poster Promos

Invite students to make posters intended to persuade viewers to subscribe to a point of view. Examples of topics that students may feel strongly about, one way or another:

- curfews for kids under age 18
- access to Web sites
- homework
- hunting season
- school uniforms
- laws about noise

Suggest to students that they rough-draft their posters with these standards in mind:

- A big, central picture can summarize the opinion visually.
- The most persuasive words and phrases should stand out through size, special lettering, eye-catching color, or position.
- Persuasive posters are not overloaded with words. They are brief because they are meant to catch, for a moment only, the attention of readers who are just passing by.

Display students' posters. Ask the class to critique them by telling how they fulfill the standards above.

4. Critiquing Commercials

As an activity to carry out at home, students and their families can view three TV commercials to analyze persuasive techniques. Give students copies of the reproducible on page 44 and preview the data they are to provide. Suggest to students that they preview the prompts and questions with their families.

Back in the classroom, have students share and compare their data. You might also ask students:

- What were you able to teach your family about persuasive techniques?
- What details and observations did your family pick up that added to your knowledge of persuasive techniques?

PICTURES, SYMBOLS, AND SLOGANS

Pictures and Slogans	What I Think Of
(smiley face)	
LIMITED SUPPLY!	
(Statue of Liberty)	
You Are a Winner!	
(dog)	
Open Immediately!	
(umbrella)	

TRANSFER TECHNIQUES

Feeling, Emotion	Picture or Catchphrase	What the Advertiser Is Selling
1. Wanting to be healthy		
2. Loving your pets		
3. Wanting to be popular and up-to-date		
4. Caring about your family		
5. Wanting to save money		
6. Wanting to do well in school		

Name _____

CRITIQUING COMMERCIALS

	Techniques Used	Channel / Date / Time
Commercial #1 **PRODUCT OR SERVICE:**		
Commercial #2 **PRODUCT OR SERVICE:**		
Commercial #3 **PRODUCT OR SERVICE:**		

PART THREE

PERSUADING FOR DIFFERENT PURPOSES

GETTING STARTED

Through activities in Parts One and Two, students have identified and practiced using the elements and techniques of persuasive writing. Part Three activities help students apply what they've learned to write persuasively in many different situations. Whatever the situation, the same guidelines generally apply. Ahead of time, prepare the following **SAY IT** poster for display and remind students to refer to it as they write.

Guidelines for Persuasive Writing

S STATE YOUR **S**UBJECT.

A KNOW YOUR **A**UDIENCE.

Y IDENTIFY **Y**OURSELF.

I KNOW YOUR **I**NTENTION. WHY ARE YOU WRITING?

T DECIDE ON THE **T**ONE.

ANALYZE A MODEL

Applying Guidelines

This activity introduces the class to the guidelines above.

Procedure

1. Ahead of time, write the following paragraph on the chalkboard or reproduce it to show on the overhead projector.

> **A Name of Your Own**
>
> If you don't like your name, you should have the right to choose a new one. As a child who at birth was named Ebeneezer Cratchinottom Pelonious Smithwhithers, I can attest to the importance of this right. If all of us who do not like our names form a committee, we may be able to convince lawmakers to make Name Change a guaranteed right of kids over the age of eight.

2. Ask the class to point out how the paragraph adheres to the guidelines. Examples:

S What is the subject? (the right to change your name)
A Who is the audience? (people who don't like their names)
Y Writer, identify yourself! (someone who doesn't like his name)
 I What is the writer's intention? (to form a committee to push for a name-change law)
T What is the tone? (serious, urgent)

3. Point out that the sample paragraph can be followed by one or more paragraphs that develop the subject with supporting ideas and facts. Ask the class to brainstorm for some of these. List students' suggestions. Examples:

- A survey shows that _____% of kids in our school don't like their names.
- Older people have a right to change their names, so why not younger people?
- Your name should express your view of yourself and how you want other people to react to you.
- Committees can bring about change more effectively than can individuals working alone.

WRITE

Ask students to work independently or with a partner to write a persuasive paragraph to open an argument **for** or **against** one of the following ideas:

- Weekend curfews for teenagers
- Students in school using beepers or cell phones
- Building a new shopping mall
- Requiring all students to learn a second language
- Setting up a dress-code for all students
- Requiring all students to take courses in music and art

Ask students to use the SAY IT guidelines as they write their paragraphs, and ask the classroom audience to check for adherence to these guidelines as they hear the paragraphs read aloud. Writers may wish to revise their paragraphs to incorporate audience feedback. Remind writers and their audience that their paragraphs are opening paragraphs. Supporting ideas and details would be presented in subsequent paragraphs. Some of your writers might want to get classmates' input about what these follow-up paragraphs might include.

WRITING EDITORIALS AND LETTERS

Through this activity, students practice using persuasive strategies in addressing a large audience of readers.

What You'll Need
For the overhead, copies of the reproducible on page 57, a selection of editorials and letters to the editor that have appeared recently in local and national newspapers (Ideally you'll find examples that deal with four or five different issues important to your students, and that present persuasive arguments for different sides of each issue. Group the examples in Subject Folders for students to use in Step 3.)

Procedure
1. Show page 57 on the overhead. Explain that an editorial is a brief essay written by an editor of the newspaper to express the point of view of the newspaper's management. After you or a student reads the editorial aloud, ask the class to critique it:

- How does the editorial adhere to the SAY IT guidelines?
- What facts and examples support the point of view?

Use underlining and write notes in the margin to record apt responses. Also ask why an editorial writer uses the word *we* instead of *I*.

2. Explain that the letters express the opinions of individuals about the issue covered in the editorial. Students read the letters on page 57 aloud and then critique them as they did the editorial. (See 1, above.) Which letter follows the SAY IT guidelines **and** uses supporting facts and examples? (letter 1). What is missing in letter 2? (supporting facts and examples)

3. Divide the class into four or five Critique Groups. Each group works with a Subject Folder you've prepared for *What You'll Need*. Group members read the folder contents and then discuss the following:

- Which argument is presented most persuasively? Why?
- Which argument is least persuasive? Why?

Act as a mentor by sitting in on groups' discussions. If necessary, help students pinpoint specific words and phrases in the editorials and letters that back up their answers to the two questions above.

WRITE

Ask students to work independently or with a partner to write an editorial on a current issue—local, regional, or global—about which they have strong feelings and opinions. (Some possible issues and points of view are listed below.)

Writers read their draft to a small group of classmates. The audience listens to determine whether the editorial follows the guidelines. Post revised editorials on a bulletin board. Encourage students to write and post letters to the editor that support or counter the editorial opinion.

TOPICS	EDITORIAL OPINION
• In-line skaters	Don't allow them to use sidewalks.
• Rural roads	Widen them to allow more traffic.
• School truants	Fine parents when kids skip school.
• Abandoned pets	Put them to sleep at the Animal Shelter.
• Internet Chat Rooms	Kids should have access to all of them.

WRITING CRITICAL REVIEWS: BOOK REVIEWS

Critiquing a Book

In general, a book report simply supplies data. A book review, on the other hand, analyzes and evaluates a work of literature and tells the reviewer's opinion of it.

What You'll Need

For the overhead projector, a copy of the reproducible on page 58; for each student, copies of the same reproducible

Procedure

1. Start with a discussion of word meanings.

EVERYDAY TALK:

Criticize and **Criticism** usually mean pointing out the negative points. Examples: *He criticized my clothes by saying they were out-of-date. His constant criticism of my clothes made me feel awful.* Ask students to suggest other sentences in which *criticize* and *criticism* mean negative reactions.

THE LANGUAGE OF REVIEWERS:

Criticize, **Criticism**, **Critique**, and **Critical** mean analyzing and evaluating something, stressing the strong, positive points as well as any weak points. Examples: *She helped me criticize (or critique) my story to see whether one event leads to the next one. Her criticism showed me that my story is logical. In her critical review, she praised the way I develop the personality of the main character in my story. Her critique also suggested that the story setting was too vague.*

To reinforce the "language of reviewers," ask the class to suggest ways to complete the following sentences:

- I'll write a *critical* review of my favorite book.
- Your *criticism* of my story helped me, because you pointed out _____.
- Please help me *critique* (or *criticize*) my editorial to make sure I've followed the guidelines for _____.

2. Distribute the copies of page 58 and preview the guidelines for writing book reviews. As you or a student reads the book review aloud, the class listens to determine how and where each guideline is followed. Discuss students' reactions and responses. To whom would this review be particularly helpful? What else would you like the reviewer to tell you about?

WRITE

Distribute the copies of page 59. Ask each student to choose a book she or he has read and supply the data asked for on the form.

Next, ask students to use the completed form as a guide for writing a draft of a book review. At this point, you may wish to present the Composition Skill activity on page 54, *Using Strong Openers*.

Ask students to work in groups of four or five to read their book reviews and discuss how they do or don't follow the guidelines. Reviewers note group criticisms and decide which ones they'll implement in a final copy. Students can publish revised, edited, and proofread reviews by including them in a Books We've Read folder for classmates, by presenting them in a Book Talk session in your school or local library, or by duplicating them for a Literature Update bulletin to share with families at home.

WRITING CRITICAL REVIEWS: FIELDS OF INTEREST

Writing Reviews of Places and Events
Encourage students to apply what they've learned about critiques and book reviews to write critical reviews of places and of events.

Procedure
1. Ask students to brainstorm for a list of local businesses and community events and places that they could critique. Examples:

- grocery stores
- gas stations
- fairs
- museums

- restaurants
- book stores
- playgrounds
- concerts

- clothing stores
- drugstores
- parks
- music stores

Have the class choose one or two items from the list and think of some features a critiquer should tell about. Examples:

Restaurant	County Fair
atmosphere	purpose or sponsors
type of food	kinds of rides and attractions
quality of food	transportation, parking
prices	costs and fees
service	safety, health

Reviewer's Rating:
Do you recommend this restaurant? Why or why not?

Reviewer's Rating:
Do you encourage others to go to the fair? Why or why not?

2. Have students work in groups of four. The group decides on a critique subject (for example, local restaurants), chooses two examples, forms two partner teams, and assigns one example to each team. Partners draft a critical review and then read the review aloud to the other partner team. The group confers:

• Does the critique follow the SAY IT guidelines?
• Does the critique supply specific details?
• Is the reviewer's opinion or rating clear?
• Is one critique more convincing than the other? If so, why?

Ask group members to discuss ways to improve the two critiques.

WRITE

Have students work independently to critique other events or places. To conference and suggest revisions, writing partners can use the four questions above as guides. To publish, students can organize their reviews into a magazine format.

A New Clothing Store

There's a new store on Main Street. It's Jan's Jeans 'n Stuff, a small shop packed with many name brands of clothing and shoes.

My friends and I visited the store on opening day to see if it carried our favorite kind of athletic shoes, Road Hogs. No such luck, but we did find racks and shelves packed with the kinds of T-shirts, jeans, caps, and baseball jackets we like. The prices are a little higher than they are at Soupy Savers. However, Soupy Savers doesn't have the variety that Jan's Jeans does. Also, we were impressed by the great service at Jan's. The clerks are polite and helpful. If you're looking for the latest in casual clothes, I suggest you give Jan's a try.

WRITING A PERSUASIVE ESSAY

Writing Process Steps

Essay is a broad term which refers to a short composition on a single subject. In a persuasive essay, the writer states his or her point of view on a subject and gives reasons for holding this point of view. The following activity leads students through the steps for writing a four-paragraph essay.

What You'll Need

For the overhead projector, a copy of the sample essay on page 64, copies of the reproducible on page 60

Procedure

1. Introduce the activity by explaining what a persuasive essay is and then by briefly reviewing the skills your students have acquired that will help them write the essay successfully. Examples:

- stating your subject clearly
- stating your opinion
- using logic and reasoning
- choosing a tone
- identifying yourself
- using facts and examples
- considering your audience
- using exact, vivid words

2. To help students concentrate on essay content, show page 64 on the overhead. Walk the class through the essay; after you or a student has read a paragraph aloud, pause to get students' input about persuasive skills and guidelines the writer has used in that paragraph. Build an I-Can-Do-That-Too atmosphere by reminding students again that they've already practiced and applied each skill.

3. Distribute the copies of page 60. Explain that the outline shows the form of the persuasive essay. With students, critique the sample essay on the overhead to point out how it follows the form.

4. Ask students to work with partners to explore topics for their own persuasive essays. Most students will find ideas and writing samples in their Writing Folders that they can develop into essays. Additional ideas can come from brainstorming and discussing hot topics in the news. Stress a further guideline: Pick a topic about which there are genuine differences of opinion. For example, few people would disagree with the opinions that water supplies should be clean, that we should be kind to animals, that young people need a good education, or that smoking is dangerous to health. However, there are real differences of opinion about who should be responsible for cleaning up water supplies, how the local animal shelter should be run, how local schools can be improved, and how to discourage people from smoking.

5. To help students choose an exciting essay subject and to think about their audience, use the *Thinking About Your Audience* activity on page 53.

WRITE

Provide several writing periods for students to plan, polish, and present their persuasive essays. As a prewriting strategy, ask students to freewrite for three or four minutes about their topic. In the freewrite, students list in any way they like all the feelings and ideas that come to them as they consider their topic. The purpose of the freewrite is simply to "loosen up"; results don't have to be shared. The drafting stage involves two steps.

Step One: Make an outline for your essay. (Ask students to follow the form on page 60.) If you wish, go over your outline with a writing partner and ask for input and suggestions. You may want to revise your outline.

Step Two: Use your outline as a guide to write your first draft of the essay. Then put the draft away for a day. Return to it and add your fresh ideas and changes. You may want to write a second draft before your conference.

• **Conference** with your writing partner. Read your essay aloud. Then ask your partner to read it aloud. Ask your partner to help you solve any specific problems you detect in your essay.

• **Revise** your essay. Work with your partner to **proofread** for errors in spelling, grammar, and punctuation. Make the **final copy** of your essay.

Have students brainstorm for ways to publish their persuasive essays. In addition to compiling an anthology, students might consider:

• Morning Analysis: Open the school day by having a student read his or her persuasive essay aloud. Provide a couple of minutes for audience commentary about the strong points of the writing, but not about whether they disagree or agree with the point of view.

• Round-Table Reviews: Group students according to the general topics they've written about—for example, the environment, television programs, problems at school. In a round-table setting before the class, have these students briefly present their persuasive arguments orally, using their essay outlines as guides.
   (Suggested ground rules: Go one at a time. Keep your presentation brief [about two minutes]. Don't interrupt.)

For a follow-up discussion, the audience makes notes about strong and weak points in each presentation.

Note that the two publishing strategies above also provide you, the teacher, with opportunities to assess and evaluate students' persuasive writing skills.

Planning Counterarguments

In the activity on page 17, *Analyzing Different Viewpoints*, students objectively listed pro and con positions on an issue. The following activity extends the concept and skill for your students: they not only try to *predict* the supporting reasons for an opposing point of view but also plan how to *counter* these reasons as they write their persuasive paragraphs or essays.

What You'll Need

For each student, copies of the reproducible on page 61; a copy of the same reproducible for the overhead

---

PROS AND CONS ABOUT HOMEWORK

1. Our Position: Our school should have a No-Homework policy. Here are our supporting reasons for our point of view:

- The school day can be organized so that kids get all their work done in class.
- Many kids have a home environment that makes studying real hard to do.
- Most homework is just drill, practice, and repetition.
- Kids need free time at home to relax, to enjoy their friends and family, and to pursue their own interests.

2. Our Opponent's Position: Here are our opponent's reasons for supporting a Pro-Homework policy:

- By doing homework, kids learn to think and work independently.
- Many school research assignments can only be carried out away from school.
- By discussing homework with their families, students show families what they are learning at school.

3. Counterarguments: Here are our group's ideas for countering, or answering, the arguments and supporting reasons in 2.

Procedure

1. Distribute the copies of page 61. Ask students to work in groups of five or six. Explain the task:

- In Box 1, the group lists at least three reasons to support a No-Homework policy. Explain that while groups are working, you'll list on a piece of paper at least three reasons to support a Pro-Homework policy.
- After group members complete Box 1, they confer to predict what reasons *you* may have listed to support a Pro-Homework policy. The group enters its predictions in Box 2.

2. Read to your class the way one class and an opponent filled in boxes 1 and 2 (see above). (While students may wish to tell how their groups' entries tally with the examples, stress that different entries may also be valid.) Then work with the class to respond to Our Opponent's Position by phrasing statements (counterarguments) for Box 3. Ask students to write the counterarguments in Box 3 on page 61. Examples:

- Schools can organize study halls where kids can work independently on assignments.
- Families can learn about kids' work through report cards and parent-teacher conferences.
- Research assignments can be based on what students can find out together in school, using school resources like the library and talks by school visitors.

3. Show page 62 on the overhead. Discuss how the underlined sentences and phrases predict and respond to the opposition's point of view and supporting reasons. Discuss how while we can't always exactly predict everything the opposition may say, we can make some good guesses and cover them in our persuasive writing.

Also use the essay as a model that follows the outline for a persuasive essay (page 60).

WRITE

Ask students to work with a partner. Distribute copies of page 63. Preview the prompts, and present the activity as a "trial run," that is, not for publication.

- Partners use the prompts and their responses to draft a persuasive essay, using the model on page 64 as a model for organization.
- Partners reflect on the writing task: What was difficult about it? What was easy?
- Partners read their work aloud to another partner-group. Groups discuss the "hard" and "easy" parts and suggest ways to solve the former.

COMPOSITION SKILL: USING STRONG OPENERS

1. Ahead of time, copy the following list on the chalkboard. Ask students to match each sentence in column 1 with the sentence in column 2 that introduces the same topic. Which sentences are more interesting and audience-grabbing?

Opening Sentences

• Delivery trucks should not be allowed to double-park.	• What's holding up traffic down the block?
• We need art and music classes in our middle school.	• Just look at the stories whir neatly out of the ink-jet printer!
• Handwriting lessons are old fashioned and unnecessary.	• The new school budget cuts out the classes my friends and I like most.

2. Help students analyze the opening sentences in column 2. The first is a question, the second an exclamation, and the third a statement that sets the reader wondering "What are the classes?"

3. Ask the class to brainstorm a list of persuasive writing topics, perhaps using Writing Folders as a source of ideas. Students then choose one of the topics and work together to compose different opening sentences. Write the sentences on the chalkboard and ask the class to decide which one they like best and to explain their choice. Repeat this procedure with two or three other topics.

4. Suggest to students that they include opening sentences among the things they consider as they draft their editorials and book reviews. Also suggest that students look for strong opening sentences in newspaper and magazine articles, and for headlines that state main ideas in an audience-grabbing way.

ADDITIONAL ACTIVITIES

1. A Debate Between Book Characters

Ask students to work with a partner. Partners choose two characters from two different books or stories and imagine them debating an issue or exchanging opinions. Examples:

Characters	Talk About
The wolf from "Little Red Riding Hood" and the fox from "The Fox and the Grapes"	the best meal
Aladdin and Jason (or another mythic hero or heroine)	who is braver
Billie Wind (*Talking Earth*) and Julie (*Julie of the Wolves*)	the scariest adventure

Partners can present the debate as a written conversation, or set it up as dialogue for a skit. Ask students to apply the SAY IT guidelines as they develop the debate.

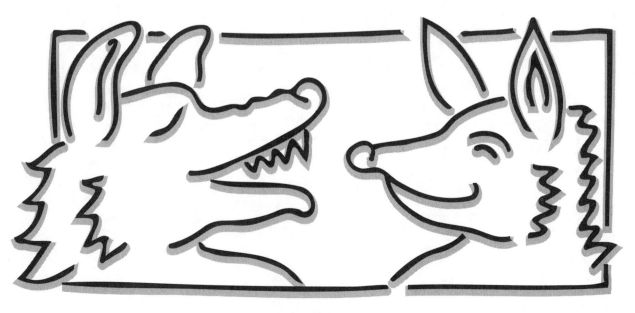

2. Using Visuals

Discuss with students the saying "One picture is worth a thousand words." Have students seen photographs that helped persuade them to adopt a certain point of view (for example, photos of starving children; of forest land destroyed by fire)? Ask students to look through newspapers and magazines to find and clip examples of photos and pictures that are meant to influence the audience's opinion on an issue. Students can write brief caption critiques of the visuals to explain what makes them persuasive.

3. Detecting Argument Fallacies

As an activity to carry out with families at home, students can watch television discussion shows to detect any the following common "argument fallacies":

• The Missing the Point fallacy: The speaker expresses an opinion, but then offers facts that have nothing to do with that opinion. For example: The residents need flood relief immediately. This is a wonderful part of the country, and our governor is a fine man.

• The Ad Hominem fallacy: The speaker doesn't address the issue, but instead attacks his or her opponent personally. For example: I disagree with you about school uniforms. You're a dangerous person who's always trying to change everything.

• Circular reasoning: The speaker tries to support an idea by stating the same idea in a different way. For example: You should eat healthy foods because they're good for you. The reason they're good for you is because they're healthy.

4. Defending a Personal Choice

Talk with students about the fact that some choices do not have to be defended, because they're a matter of personal taste. Examples: a favorite color, sport, food, type of music, book. Ask students to choose one of the examples and write a poem to explain why it's a personal favorite.

EDITORIAL AND LETTERS-TO-THE-EDITOR

EDITORIAL

To what extent should drivers of all-terrain vehicles determine how our woodlands are used? This is a question that concerns all of us who like to explore the Catskill Mountains. Here at the *Mountain Post*, we believe that our forests and hills attract residents and tourists who like hiking through the wild, untouched beauty and silence of the woods and hills. We feel that all-terrain vehicles destroy these attractions. The vehicles are noisy. Drivers cut muddy paths through forests, destroying plants and frightening animals away. The question of access to our woodlands is currently before our state legislators. We urge all of you who love the wildness of our mountains to write to our state representatives. Urge them to conserve our hills by prohibiting vehicles.

1. To the Editor:

Your comments about all-terrain vehicles in woodlands are way off-base! First of all, state parks are open to everyone, and there's no law on the books that says drivers can't use the parks. Second, most of the drivers I know are really careful not to disturb or destroy wild growth and animal habitats.

As for noise, I don't think vehicles make any more noise than do hikers who are always talking and yelling. Also, drivers who go into remote areas of the mountains often find lost hikers or dangerous situations. Like lifeguards, we report these situations to Park Rangers.

Tiry Wheelgood
Petunsquet, New York

2. To the Editor:

My family enjoys using mountain bikes and ski-mobiles in the hills. We don't agree with your editorial. Other people who feel as we do should write to their state representatives.

Ike Biker
Snowville, New York

BOOK REVIEWS

GUIDELINES FOR WRITING A BOOK REVIEW

1. Tell the title of the book, the author's name, and the reviewer's name. (For example, State your **S**ubject and tell who **Y**ou, the reviewer, are.)
2. Start with a sentence that grabs your audience's attention. (For example, Know your **A**udience.)
3. Supply details:
   - What is the book about?
   - If you've read other books by this writer, tell how this book is like or unlike them.
   - State the theme the book: What message or idea is the writer trying to persuade readers to agree to?
4. Know your **I**ntention. Are you recommending this book for everyone to read? just for classmates with special interests? to no one, because you think the book has serious flaws?
5. Decide on a **T**one for your report. Will you be serious? funny? informal? formal? worried? happy?

KIDS AT WORK, by Russell Freedman
Reviewer: Charles Reeder

Do you think history is boring? You'll change your mind when you read Russell Freedman's *Kids At Work: Lewis Hine and the Crusade Against Child Labor*. This nonfiction book tells about how thousands of kids had to do back-breaking labor in mills, mines, and factories, and how Lewis Hine, a reporter and photographer, recorded the work kids did.

Russell Freedman is well-known for his ability to tell about history in personal ways. For example, in *The Wright Brothers*, Freedman tells how Orville and Wilbur Wright felt when their first attempts at manned-flights failed. In *Kids At Work*, Freedman shows how frustrated Hine became as he tried to get his message across to the public that young children should be in school, not in sweatshops. Yet, the theme of this book is that courage and perseverance eventually pay off. After many years, Hine's photos and articles led to child-labor laws.

Kids At Work is not an easy book to read, because Freedman doesn't talk down to his audience. But the book will be valuable to you if you're interested in the problems kids faced many years ago. You can also learn a lot just by looking at Hine's great photographs.

Name _____

CRITIQUING A BOOK

MY PLAN FOR A BOOK REVIEW

1. (Book title) _____

2. A _____ **by** _____
   (**Genre**: for example, novel, biography,   (author's name)
   science book, memoir, science fiction story)

3. What audience might be especially interested in this kind of book?
_____

Write an opening sentence to grab the audience's attention.
_____

4. In one sentence, summarize what the book is about.
_____

5. In one or two sentences, tell what other books the author has written and/or
   what other stories this book is like. _____
_____

6. Who are the main characters? _____
_____

7. What is the setting? _____
_____

8. What is the theme, or main idea, the writer tries to get across? _____
_____

9. In your opinion, what are the weak points of the book? _____
_____

10. In your opinion, what are the strong points of the book? _____
_____

11. Will you encourage your friends to read this book? Tell why or why not.
_____

OUTLINE FOR A PERSUASIVE ESSAY

I. Introductory Paragraph

A. State your subject and your intention in writing about it. Identify yourself and the audience you're addressing.

B. Give **two** reasons that support your argument.

C. State your opinion in just a sentence or two.

II. Development Paragraph

A. Restate the **first** reason that supports your point of view.

B. Write sentences that give examples and details that support this reason.

III. Development Paragraph

A. Restate the **second** reason that supports your point of view.

B. Write sentences that give examples and details that support this reason.

IV. Concluding Paragraph

A. Restate the subject of your essay.

B. Summarize how your reasons support your point of view.

C. Conclude with a summary of your opinion.

Name _____

PROS AND CONS ABOUT HOMEWORK

1. Our Position: Our school should have a No-Homework policy. Here are our supporting reasons for our point of view:

_____
_____
_____
_____
_____
_____
_____
_____

2. Our Opponent's Position: Here are our opponent's reasons for supporting a Pro-Homework policy:

_____
_____
_____
_____
_____
_____
_____
_____
_____

3. Counterarguments: Here are our group's ideas for countering, or answering, the arguments and supporting reasons in 2.

_____
_____
_____
_____
_____
_____
_____
_____

HOMEWORK: YES OR NO?

A debate is raging about the value of homework for students in our school system. This debate involves <u>a conflict between students, teachers, and parents</u>. As a student in Room 10 at Flora Daski Middle School, I'm pro-homework. Homework takes up a lot of my time, but it also encourages me to develop my interests and to get my family involved in interesting projects.

I have some interests that are tied into school subjects. One of my main interests is collecting historical, antique American coins and paper money. <u>Opponents of homework may think I can pursue this interest at school</u>, but actually I rely on school history lessons to inspire after-school quests for rare items that I could never find at school! For example, our teacher assigned our class to find examples of things used in pre-revolutionary days in America. So after school I went to the local historical museum and found examples of paper money used in Thomas Jefferson's day. Away from school, I found examples to show to my classmates.

<u>Some opponents of homework claim that it interferes with free-time with your family</u>. Actually, I've found that an interesting homework assignment can get you **more** involved with your family. For example, the homework assignment to find persuasive strategies in TV commercials got my whole family involved in critiquing commercials. We had fun detecting persuasive techniques and shared a lot of ideas as we discussed them.

In conclusion, I support homework assignments that help you go on learning away from school. <u>Opponents of homework don't realize that learning is not confined to the classroom</u>. I vote for homework that encourages my interests and helps me and my family learn together!

Name _____

Partners' names _____

PERSUASIVE ESSAY PLAN

1. **Choose an issue:** _____
_____

2. **State your position (your point of view) on this issue.**
_____
_____
_____

3. **State the point of view of your opponent.**
_____
_____
_____

4. **List ideas and facts that support your point of view.**
_____
_____
_____
_____
_____

5. **List ideas and facts your opponent might use.**
_____
_____
_____
_____

6. **Write sentences that counter your opponent's ideas.**
_____
_____
_____
_____

SAMPLE MODEL ESSAY

Mall Manners

Like most other people in our community, I like the stores, food court, and CinePlex at Mathis Mall. But one problem at the mall has been a bunch of rowdy kids. The mall management has just hired two Roving Ambassadors to help solve the problem. I support the management's decision. The rowdy kids scare shoppers and make them angry. Also, most of the kids involved are really insecure and are looking for someone to respect them.

Most of us who go to the mall want to shop and eat in peace. We don't like to be alarmed or threatened by kids who are pushing, shoving, skating, hollering, and running around bumping into people. In fact, this kind of behavior makes some of us shoppers so angry that we stop going to the mall. The Roving Ambassadors will solve this problem by spotting troublemakers and escorting them outside.

Both Roving Ambassadors are people who like kids and understand their problems. Some kids just need an adult who will tell them what the rules are. Mall rules are simple: come here only to shop, eat, or see movies. Some kids also need to find positive ways of getting attention. The Roving Ambassadors will point out some positive ways, like opening doors for elderly people, and cleaning up after oneself at the food court.

Malls are designed to be inviting to everyone in the community. Roving Ambassadors will keep our mall peaceful by identifying troublemakers and taking them aside. The ambassadors will help these kids by stating rules and by sharing ideas about how to get attention in ways that get praise, not blame. I think the idea of Roving Ambassadors is one that will benefit all of us.